I0021682

MANAGING YOUR DIGITAL ASSETS

MANAGING YOUR DIGITAL ASSETS

To all my family and friends that encouraged me to find my way through life regardless of the challenges I faced.

To my children who I love with all my heart, and wish that they will forever know that love for themselves.

To my partner who stands by everything I do with an eager anticipation to help in any way possible.

And to the countless others that I have helped with numerous technical problems that provided the material for me to write this book.

And to all that find value in these pages.

Thank You.

Ben Rusk, 2019

Acknowledgements

This being my first book I would like to thank my employers that believed enough in me to hire me, and give me the wonderful experiences in the computer science field.

Next, I would like to thank the many co-workers that I learned so much from over the years.

Next, I would like to many customers that trusted me with their businesses and implemented my advice and utilized my services to successfully operate and grow their businesses.

I would also like to thank the friends I have gathered along the way and continue to be a great influence in my life still to this day.

And I would like to thank what will hopefully be my many readers who will find value in the words I share in this book and hopefully recommend to others.

Thank You.

MANAGING YOUR DIGITAL ASSETS

Contents

MANAGING YOUR DIGITAL ASSETS

Preface

Honey! What's the password to our Netflix account?

I don't remember!

Damn, now I need to reset the password again!!!

How many times have you gone through this cycle?

Time and time again we forget or misplace valuable data which is critical to getting things done.

When is someone going to develop a process to once and for all end the vicious cycle of FORGOT PASSWORD?

1. Enter your email address
2. Check your inbox for the email just sent
3. Click here to reset password
4. Enter NEW password
5. Now do it again with no special characters
6. Passwords don't match
7. Your password has successfully been changed!

Hopefully, this book will reduce if not put an end to all that.

Take you time and get your digital assets under control.

Introduction

After 32 years of working with computers it is still surprising to me how many people just trust a computer to do the right thing.

After helping hundreds of people recover and organize many files it just seems natural that I write this book to help the thousands more that need this same help.

We need to take control of our digital assets and put them in a logical place so we know where to find them next time.

Remember the toy box - and our parents telling us if we didn't put our toys away, they were going to get lost. What they meant was taken away.

Well, the same is true with computers and other devices. If we do not put our data (digital assets) in a safe place (toy box) and something unthinkable happens, it will all be taken away.

I once stored a very precious memory on an external hard-drive which was given to me and I thought it was a very safe place to store my most treasured digital asset (pictures of my children growing up). Then one day an electrical storm caused the device to stop working.

MANAGING YOUR DIGITAL ASSETS

I was panicking beyond belief. I called around to every resource I knew to call. Data Recovery was going to costs me $1500 and up to 3 months due to their backlog. I did not care - I would pay any price to recover that data.

Fortunately, I got it all back. Whew!

But from that point forward I knew the importance of protecting my digital assets.

That is my inspiration for writing this book.

My hope is to protect you from my horrible experience and see to it that you have some guidance in how to go about storing your digital assets.

Chapter 1

Disks & Tapes

Disks & Tapes are now considered OBSOLETE. However, you may still have some of these lying around. You need to get these transferred IMMEDIATELY.

You may be asking "Why?" The answer is they are oxidizing and your data will soon be lost.

Here is a short list of disks and tapes you should be concerned with.

5.25 Floppy Disk

3.5 Floppy Disks

Cassette Tapes

MANAGING YOUR DIGITAL ASSETS

Zip Disks

Other Video Tapes

VHS Video Tapes

If you still have the equipment to transfer this data to a solid-state drive (a.k.a. Thumb Drive) or other permanent storage you should do so as soon as possible.

If you do not have the equipment then you should look into buying an external USB drive that will help you with the transfer.

There are also service that will convert your media for a price.

If you have any questions on how to obtain these devices or go about the data transfer contact your local computer retailer for assistance.

Recommendations

External USB / 3.5 floppy disk drive

External USB / Zip Drive 100/250 MB

Cassette to MP3 to CD

Video to MP4 to DVD

Chapter 2

Hard Drives

Hard Drive Data is another very important asset. Where you store your data on these drives matters when it comes to data retrieval.

If you are not organized with where you store your data and you suffer a disk drive crash or worse. Then retrieving your data may be next to impossible.

Now I know there are defaults for where your software programs want to store the data you create. But they are not consistent. And the operating system you are on my even have an impact on where your data is stored.

Here is a simple way to organize your data on a PC or MAC.

1 Drive (C:) Method

Create a primary folder called MY_DATA as a container for all of the files you need to save.

Then use sub-folders to organize your data.

C:\MY_DATA

C:\MY_DATA\WORD

MANAGING YOUR DIGITAL ASSETS

C:\MY_DATA\EXCEL

C:\MY_DATA\PAYSTUBS

2 Drive (C: & D:) Method

<u>C:\ Drive</u>

Use the C: drive for your operating system and any other software you install on your computer. Be sure to save any media you used to install your software just in case you need to re-install it again.

Save the packaging that your software installation media came in as it frequently contains the KEY to register the installed software.

If you installed your software from a downloaded file then store those files in a folder called D:\MY_DATA\INSTALLS\Software Name.

Also, be sure to create a TXT file to contain any KEY to unlocking that software.

Software or Product Keys are normally a very long string of characters that may look something like this.

CCW8H-R84M8-FWXNX-X3B7V-R5FVB

Be sure to record these keys correctly or you may not be able to re-install the software when necessary.

MANAGING YOUR DIGITAL ASSETS

D:\ Drive

Use the D: drive for all files you create.

Think about all the hours you put in to create your works of art, Presentations, Documents, etc.

Use the same folder organization on the D: drive as in the single drive method described above.

While we are talking about hard drives you might even have extra drives hanging around.

If you would like to access the data on old hard drives without re-installing them into a computer then I recommend a docking station.

Be sure to order one that is right for the type of drive you have.

Chapter 3

Thumb Drives

Thumb Drives are very handy. Just as the floppy drives were in the past.

You may find that you acquire many of these little devices which come in many shapes and sizes.

So how do you keep track of what is on each of these storage devices?

You need to create an inventory list.

I suggest a using a spreadsheet to create this list.

Here are some column names you may wish to use:

- Manufacturer
- Color
- ID – This may be a mark you apply (A) (B) etc.
- Size
- Description (such as My Resumes)

It may also be a good idea to backup the data on these devices to an online storage account for safe keeping.

Here is how I would backup my thumb drives in the cloud or other online storage location.

MANAGING YOUR DIGITAL ASSETS

MY_DATA\My-Thumb-Id\Contents

Where the contents would be the data on that thumb drive.

You may also consider dating the contents.

MY_DATA\My-Thumb-Id\Date\Contents

Chapter 4

Devices

We all have devices that store an enormous amount of data without us even knowing it.

MP3 Players

Think about your MP3 player, it has hundreds of MP3 files that you have collected over the years.

Backup Software: _____

Last Backup: _____

Tablets

Then you have a tablet that has been configured for your specific preferences.

Backup Software: _____

Last Backup: _____

MANAGING YOUR DIGITAL ASSETS

Smartphones

And finally, there is your smartphone which is loaded with contact information and an endless number of apps.

Backup Software: _____

Last Backup: _____

Each of these devices should be backed up with their respective software or services.

A critical failure in one of these devices would mean the end of the data which they contain.

Purse or Wallet

And, don't forget about the cards in your wallet or purse. Credits cards, Licenses, etc.

Take a photo or scan both sides of all cards just in case your purse or wallet is lost or stolen.

Then store this digital image file in a folder for safe keeping.

Chapter 5

Online Storage

With the latest emerging technology called "Cloud Storage" there have been many services which are now promoting space in the cloud for just pennies.

These services offer protection from many of the physical world dilemmas we all face:

- Accidental Damage
- Theft
- Fire

But we all need to be aware of what we are putting in the cloud. There are no guarantees that it will remain safe forever.

Hackers are making the news more and more frequently so stop and think before you put your digital assets in the cloud.

However, there are some benefits to putting your data in the cloud. It makes it easier to share with others, and it makes it more accessible to you from various locations.

So, with any new tool be sure to read and understand the safety instructions before using.

MANAGING YOUR DIGITAL ASSETS

Be sure to record the following information so you will be able to return to your online storage account.

Service Name: _____

Service URL: _____

Setup Date: _____

Cost: _____

Login ID: _____

Password: _____

Personally, I use a physical Account & Password journal to capture and store this vital information.

MANAGING YOUR DIGITAL ASSETS

MANAGING YOUR DIGITAL ASSETS

Address & Telephone journals will work just as well.

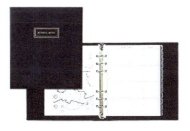

Chapter 6

Online Services

Do you ever wonder how we survived without the internet?

Today I find every hour filled with tapping my phone to check an account balance, verify a package delivery, validate a stock quote, listen to an audiobook, check the weather, schedule an appointment, jump on a webinar, hold a conference call, catch up on the latest antics of friends, find a recipe for dinner, or refill a prescription.

And the list goes on and on.

How did I ever get so connected (and reliant) on the internet?

The answer is one new thing at a time.

And how do I access all of these fantastic services you might ask? Using the computer or smartphone.

Now ask yourself this question, "What would happen if I lost my computer or smartphone?" Would I be able to regain access to all of those services again?

Truth is, NOT a chance.

MANAGING YOUR DIGITAL ASSETS

UNLESS, I back it all up in a safe file I call my "Resource Guide". This is a document where I store all of the details to access all of my online service accounts.

Here is what you need to collect for each online service account.

Service Name: _____

Service URL: _____

Setup Date: _____

Cost: _____

Renewal Date: _____

Frequency: _____

Credit Card: _____

Login ID: _____

Password: _____

Then to keep it all safe you should password protect this document as well.

Do not convert it to a PDF as you will want to add and remove resources from the list over time.

Chapter 7

Financial Accounts

Now we get to the number one most important topic of this book, your financial records.

Do you know that when you signed up for eStatements from your bank that you now own the responsibility to download those statements every month?

If you choose not to, the bank will store them for you for up to one year. After 12 months they are archived, and in order for you to retrieve those archived statements you have to pay a fee.

So, now you have to make it part of your monthly routine to download your financial statements.

Here is a list of the financial institutions you may want to capture your eStatements from.

- Employer Paystubs
- Tax Records
- Bank Accounts
- Retirement Accounts
- Social Security Accounts
- Brokerage (Stocks) Accounts
- Brokerage (Crypto) Accounts

MANAGING YOUR DIGITAL ASSETS

Once again, I will stress storing your documents in a consistent location for easy retrieval.

Remember, you will be charged a fee for each document you request from your financial institutions.

Suggestions on where you may store your documents.

C:\MY_DATA\Employer Paystubs

C:\MY_DATA\Taxes\2019

C:\MY_DATA\Retirement

C:\MY_DATA\SocSec

C:\MY_DATA\Stocks

C:\MY_DATA\Crypto

You will also want to capture your account information for these accounts as well.

Institution Name: _____

Institution URL: _____

Account Number: _____

Login ID: _____

Password: _____

Chapter 8

Medical Records

The second most important documents may be your medical records.

Can you recall all the doctors that you have seen over the years?

I am sure everyone who reads this book cannot remember all the doctors they have seen over their lifetime.

But there is not time like the present to begin to pull as much of this information together as possible.

Even if it is just to record the major dates and events that will be important to your health care providers in the future as well as your descendants that will need a family medical history one day.

Do some research and gather this information while this idea is fresh in your mind.

Contact the facility where you saw a doctor and see if they still have your records on file.

Here is a list of suggested details to capture.

MANAGING YOUR DIGITAL ASSETS

- Medical Insurance Card
- Prescription Cards (Rx, Vision, Dental)
- Shots / Dates
- Surgery / Dates
- Diagnosis / Dates
- Treatments / Dates
- Prescriptions / Names / Amount / Dates / Purpose
- Doctors / Name / Facility / Dates
- Emergency Room Visits / Dates / Reason
- Broken Bones / Dates
- Fevers / Dates
- Symptoms / Descriptions / Photo / Dates (Skin Disorder)

You may have other recurring aches and pains which you may want to track as well.

Make this list work for you I just encourage you to make it a priority to collect this information.

With memory loss growing nation wide for many reasons one day you will thank me for calling this to your attention now.

Chapter 9

Other Important Documents

In this chapter I wanted to include the other miscellaneous documents that should also be captured in a safe place.

Some folks may feel these are more or less important but they are worth mentioning.

I know it is hard to consider what will happen when we pass from this life, but for those that you leave behind it will be helpful for them to know what you have and its value when they have to decide what to keep and treasure and what to let go.

Here are my suggestions for you to consider.

- Will, Living Will, Care Directive, Medical POA, Do Not Resuscitate (DNR)
- Power of Attorney
- Family Tree Information (Names, Photos, Documents)
- List of Assets (Personal Property) / Desc / Value / Location

MANAGING YOUR DIGITAL ASSETS

- Insurance Forms, Contracts, Service Agreements, Warranties, Coupons, Letters of Adjustment, Disputes
- Safety Deposit Boxes / Location / Key / Account
- Safe / Combination
- Lockbox / Combination or Keys

And here are some other odds and ends.

- Car Accidents (Location, Photos)
- Houses Owned (Address, Photo)
- Cars Owned (Year, Make, Model)
- Pets (Names, Photos)

In this book I have provided many examples of what is a digital asset. Is this a complete list? Not at all.

But now more than ever, you are better educated on what they are, and how to store them for safe keeping.

As the world becomes more and more digital you need to be more diligent in **Managing Your Digital Assets**.

About the Author

Ben Rusk

Ben has spent a 32-year career in information technology, earned many certifications in data processing and recently obtained credentials in Cyber Security.

He also coaches business owners on business strategies using the latest online resources to sell more products and services, for more money, to more customers, more often, for less cost.

If you are looking for a business coach go to https://www.benrusk.com for more details.

www.ingramcontent.com/pod-product-compliance
Lightning Source LLC
Chambersburg PA
CBHW041155050326
40690CB00004B/577